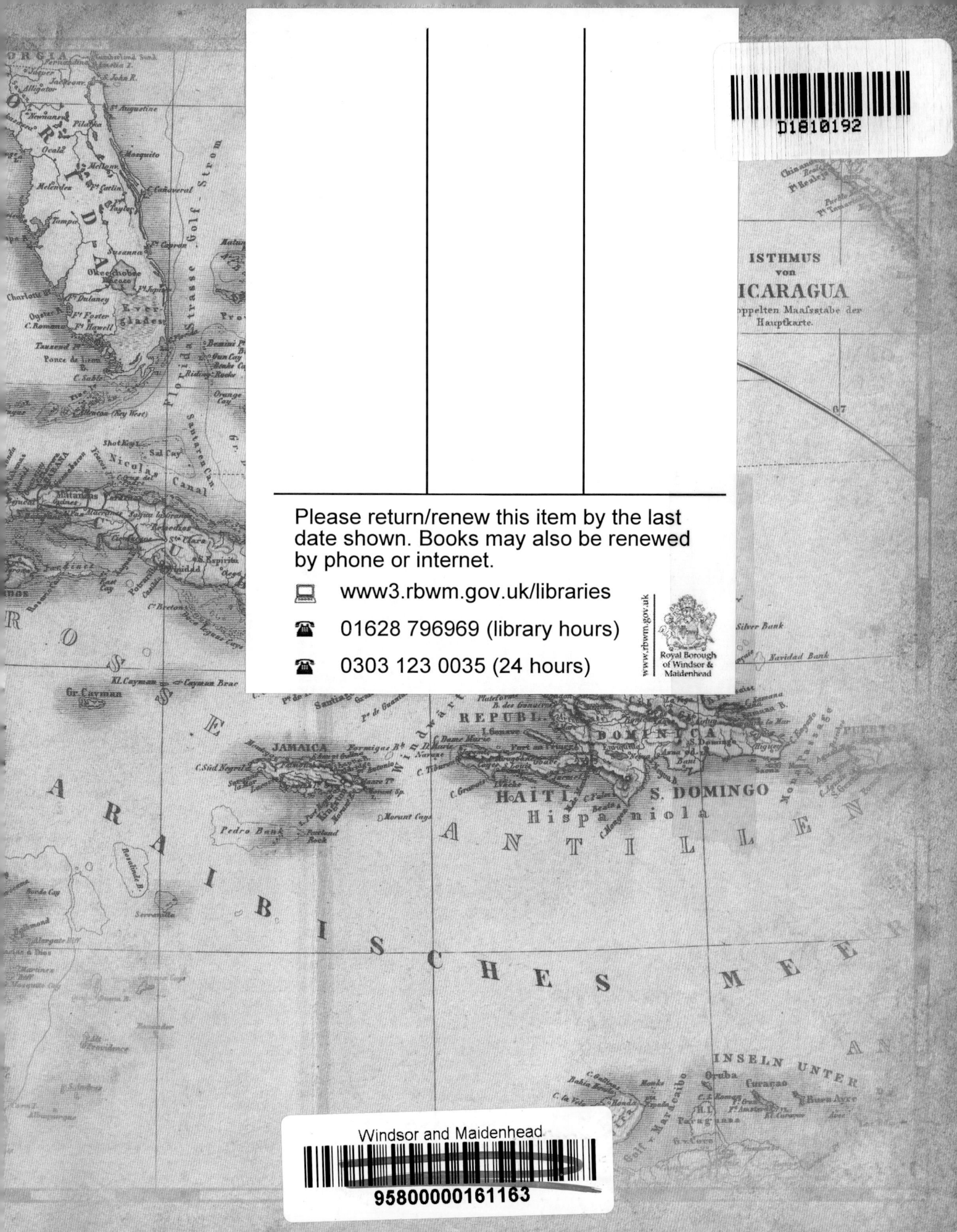

Please return/renew this item by the last date shown. Books may also be renewed by phone or internet.

www3.rbwm.gov.uk/libraries

01628 796969 (library hours)

0303 123 0035 (24 hours)

WEST-INDIEN
und
CENTRAL-AMERIKA

gezeichnet von Hermann Berghaus.

Maaſsstab = 1 / 9 250 000

Schrift Erklärung:		Europaeische Colonien:
● STADT v. über 100 000		Britische
◉ STADT - 50 000		Niederländische
● Stadt - 20 000		Schwedische
○ Stadt - 10 000		Dänische
○ Stadt - 5000		Französische
∘ Kleinere Stadt		Spanische

ISTHMUS
von
NICARAGUA

im doppelten Maaſsstabe der Hauptkarte.

LUCAISCHE oder BAHAMA INSELN

REPUBLIK

JAMAICA

HAITI S. DOMINGO

Hispaniola

DOMINICA

PUERTO

ANTILLEN

CARAIBISCHES MEER

INSELN UNTER

Resistance and Abolition

Dan Lyndon-Cohen

FRANKLIN WATTS
LONDON • SYDNEY

This edition 2020

First published in 2010 by Franklin Watts

Copyright © The Watts Publishing Group 2010

Editor: Tracey Kelly
Series editor: Adrian Cole
Art director: Jonathan Hair
Design: Stephen Prosser
Picture research: Diana Morris

Dan Lyndon-Cohen would like to thank the following people for their support in writing this book; The Black and Asian Studies Association (BASA), Marika Sherwood, Arthur Torrington, Joanna Cohen and Joanna Caroussis. Thanks also to the Lyndon, Robinson, Cohen and Childs families.

This series is dedicated to the memory of Kodjo Yenga.

Acknowledgements:

Anti-Slavery International: 35, 39b. Art Media/HIP/Topfoto: 23b. Bibliotheque Nationale Paris/Bridgeman Art Library: 21bl. Reproduced with the permission of Birmingham Libraries and Archives: 34b. Bridgeman Art Library: 25t. British Library/Topfoto: 28. Mary Evans PL: 10, 23t, 30, 37b. Faberfoto/Shutterstock: 6. Fitzwilliam Museum Cambridge/Bridgeman Art Library: 29b. Getty Images: 29t. The Granger Collection/Topfoto: front cover l, back cover r, 8bl, 8tr, 9, 13, 14t, 17, 19t, 19b, 22, 26, 32, 39c. Houses of Parliament archives: 25b. Roger Howard/PD: 18. Library of the Religious Society of Friends: 34t. LOC Washington/Bridgeman Art Library: 31tr. Nanny Maroon Hills Productions: 20. NARA: 15t. National Maritime Museum: 24. New Haven Historical Society: 14b. PC/Peter NewarkAmerican Pictures/Bridgeman Art Library: 16. Photos12/Alamy: 15b. Private Collection/Bridgeman Art Library: 11, 27t, 38. Roger-Viollet/Topfoto: 12. Royal Geographical Society/Bridgeman Art Library: 21tr. Shutterstock: front cover1, back cover r. Eileen Tweedy/Art Archive: 5, 37t. Whitworth Art Gallery Manchester: 27b. Wilberforce House Hull City Museums & Art Galleries/Bridgeman Art Library: 31bl, 33t, 33b, 36.

Every attempt has been made to clear copyright.

Should there be any inadvertent omission please apply to the publisher for rectification.

PB ISBN: 978 1 4451 8084 7
eBook ISBN: 978 1 4451 8085 4

Printed in Dubai

Franklin Watts is a division of Hachette Children's Books, an Hachette UK company.
Carmelite House
50 Victoria Embankment
London, EC4Y 0DZ
www.hachette.co.uk

Contents

Introduction

Throughout the brutal history of the Transatlantic Slave Trade that took place between the 16th and 19th centuries, Africans resisted enslavement at different times and in many ways.

Ways of resistance

This resistance included African villagers who attacked European slave ships to rescue African men, women and children destined for the plantations of the Americas and the Caribbean. Brave individuals led uprisings or escaped from the plantations and joined the 'Underground Railroad' in search of freedom. But also, in desperation, some enslaved people felt that their only resistance was to end their lives instead of living as slaves.

▲ *Detail from* Underground Railroad, *by Charles T. Webber, shows people helping slaves to escape.*

▲ *This engraving shows the 1791 slave revolt in St Domingue (Haiti).*

Resistance through survival

However, in many ways the most powerful example of resistance came in a different form: survival. Slave owners attempted to strip away any identity or humanity of the enslaved men, women and children. This was achieved by taking away their names (slaves were often given their owner's name), by denying them their culture (African music,

▲ *An evening prayer meeting of former slaves in Virginia, USA, 1864.*

religion and languages were often banned) and treating them as chattel (property) with the constant threat of physical punishment or even death.

So, what's inside?

This book continues from *Black History: Africa and the Slave Trade*, covering a period spanning the 17th–19th centuries. It contains case studies, personal accounts and in depth studies of key events and figures. Just before you turn over, though, think about this poem by Colonel William Mallory (1826–1907), a former slave who escaped to Canada and claimed his freedom in 1859:

I've won my way to Canada,
That free and happy land;
No more in cruel slavery
Need William Mallory stand.
Fare-the-well, old master,
That's enough for me!
I'm here, in dear old Canada,
Where colored men are free.

I will not have the driver's lash
Raised high above my head;
I will not have a peck of corn
Dealt out to me for bread;
For God, in His great goodness,
Came down to Calvary
And bore the burdens of the Cross
To set His people free.
Fare-the-well, old master,
That's enough for me!
I'm here in dear old Canada,
Where colored men are free.

Resistance in Africa

Africans were often enslaved as a result of war – with prisoners being sold as slaves – or by kidnapping. Resistance against slavery ranged from the people struggling against their captors, to redesigning villages so they became harder to attack. Although there is still little research on this topic, there are sources that suggest that resistance existed right from the very beginning of the Transatlantic Slave Trade.

Queen Nzinga

One of the earliest examples of resistance took place in Angola, in south-west Africa. In 1624, Queen Nzinga, leader of the Mbundu tribe, started a series of wars with the Portuguese who had come to Angola to get slaves for their plantations in Brazil and the Caribbean. She agreed a treaty with the Portuguese, but they did not keep their side of the bargain. As a result, fighting broke out and lasted for nearly 30 years. Queen Nzinga declared that her land would be 'free', meaning that no slavery would exist there.

Protection against slavers

Although most historical records of resistance to the slave trade come from the coastal regions, there were examples of resistance further inland. Communities built defences around their villages to make them harder to attack. These included large walls and barricades. Deep ditches were also dug and filled with thorns and poisonous plants. Rivers were diverted to make them harder to sail along and some villages were even moved to forests, marshes, caves and mountainous areas, which made them less likely to be discovered.

◀ Men armed with guns raid a village to capture prisoners for the slave trade.

▲ *This engraving from 1804 shows part of a high defensive wall surrounding a village.*

Protection against kidnappers

One of the ways in which Africans resisted was by setting up warning systems to prevent kidnappings. Olaudah Equiano (who was himself kidnapped and sold into slavery) described the situation in his village in his autobiography *The Interesting Narrative* …:

"One day, as I was watching at the top of a tree in our yard, I saw one of those people come into the yard … to kidnap … Immediately on this I gave the alarm of the rogue, and he was surrounded (and tied up with rope) so that he could not escape till some of the grown people came and secured him."

Fighting back

There are also many examples of Africans fighting against the European slave traders. In 1454, the Italian explorer Alvise Cadamosto was attacked by 150 African men while on the River Gambia in Africa. Over 300 years later, similar attacks were still taking place. Abdel Kader Kane, an Islamic leader from Senegal, explained what would happen to anyone who wanted to trade in enslaved Africans:

"I repeat that if your intention is to buy (Africans) you should stay home and not come to our country anymore. Because all those who come can be assured that they will lose their life."

The most frequent examples of resistance occurred on board the slave ships, with over 400 recorded slave revolts. These included armed uprisings as well as attacks from the coast, where Africans used boats to attempt to rescue captured friends and family. Despite the fact that most uprisings were unsuccessful, it has been estimated that as a result over 1 million Africans may have been saved from being transported to the Americas.

▲ *Slave revolts on board ships were brutal and bloody.*

Serious threat

The seriousness of the slave ship uprisings and other attacks led to slave ship owners taking out insurance against 'insurrection'. They also made sure that the ship's crew were heavily armed with guns and knives, and that the African men, in particular, were chained below decks. Women were

usually not chained which meant that they could also participate in the revolts, not least by spreading information amongst the captives. Resistance also took the form of committing suicide, with many Africans throwing themselves overboard to drown rather than face life as a slave.

The Little George

One of the most successful slave revolts took place in 1730 on board the slave ship *The Little George*, which was sailing from the west coast of Africa to America with 96 slaves on board. The uprising started at 4.30 in the morning, when some of the Africans escaped from their chains and killed the three crewmen who were on watch. The captain, George Scott, and the rest of the crew were then locked away in the cabins and the ship was sailed back to the coast of Sierra Leone. When they arrived, the Africans made a deal with the captain that his crew would be freed if the Africans were also allowed to leave too.

▲ *Enslaved men attack the ship's crew in a bid for freedom. Most attempts were unsuccessful.*

Slave ship *Unity*

The records of the slave ship *Unity*, which came from Liverpool, reveal that there were a number of attempts by enslaved Africans to resist:

6 June 1770
The slaves made an insurrection which was soon quelled with the loss of two women.

26 June 1770
The slaves this day proposed making an insurrection and a few of them got off their handcuffs but were detected in time.

27 June 1770
The slaves attempted to force up the gratings in the night with a design to murder the whites or drown themselves, but were prevented by the watch.

Probably the most famous uprising took place at sea on the slave ship *Amistad* (below). On 2 July 1839, 56 enslaved Africans on board began to take over the ship led by a man called Sengbe Pieh.

▲ *The slave ship* Amistad.

◄ *A portrait of Sengbe Pieh (also called Joseph Cinqué).*

The uprising

Using a rusty nail to open up the hatches covering their deck, the enslaved Africans grabbed hold of knives that were used for cutting sugar cane and attacked the crew. Some of the crew escaped in a rowing boat, but the ship's cook and the captain were killed. Having successfully taken over the ship, Pieh now ordered the sailors to return the ship to Africa. However, the navigator tricked the Africans and ended up sailing into harbour in New York. Here, the United States Navy took control of the ship and took the Africans into custody.

The trial

The transport of slaves from Africa to the Americas was now illegal, so a trial was held in Connecticut to decide what should happen to the Africans. Should they now belong to the US Navy, or the Cuban owners of the ship, or should the Africans be allowed to go free? The main argument from the Africans' supporters was that a treaty had been signed between Spain and Britain in 1817. It made the transport of slaves from Africa to America illegal. This meant that the Africans had been kidnapped and should now be set free. The judges finally agreed that the Africans on board the *Amistad* should be freed and returned to Africa. Twenty had died in the struggle to take over the ship, but the surviving 36 Africans sailed back home in 1842.

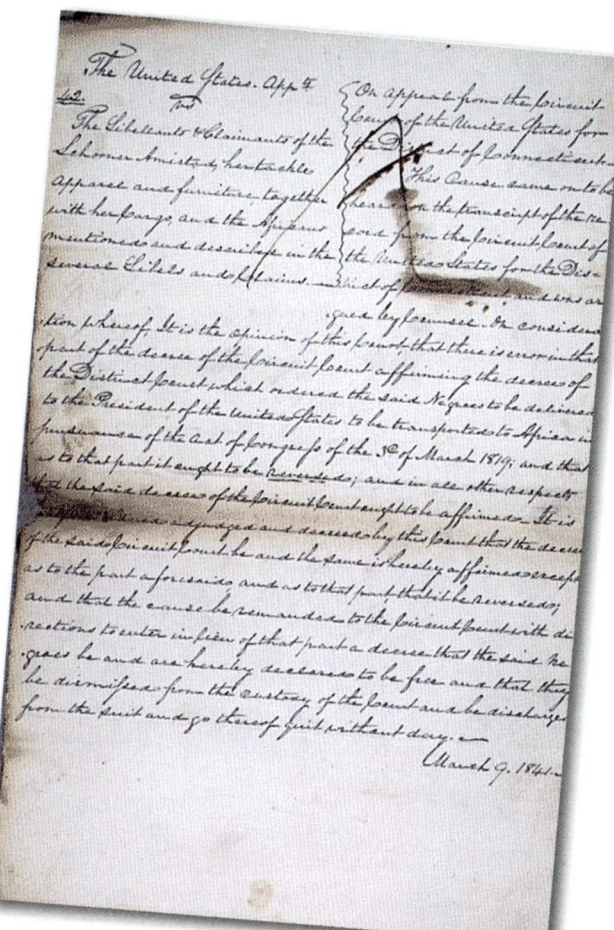

▶ *The decision of the Supreme Court US versus* Amistad, *9th March, 1841.*

Did you know?

The *Amistad* story has been made into a film, directed by Steven Spielberg, and a reconstruction of the ship was built in 2000. The Freedom Schooner *Amistad* has been sailing to ports around the world ever since, to ensure the story of the *Amistad* is remembered.

▶ *A still from Spielberg's 1997 film* Amistad.

Resistance on the plantations

The work that enslaved Africans had to do on the plantations was hard. An overseer watched constantly to make sure they kept up a high work rate, otherwise they could be whipped. Other punishments included working on treadmills, wearing iron masks or having limbs cut off. However, many Africans found ways to resist their enslavers.

Runaways

Some slaves decided to risk running away rather than stay on the plantations. Their chances of success were slim as it was difficult to find food and shelter. The slave owners sent out gangs of men with dogs to track the runaway down.

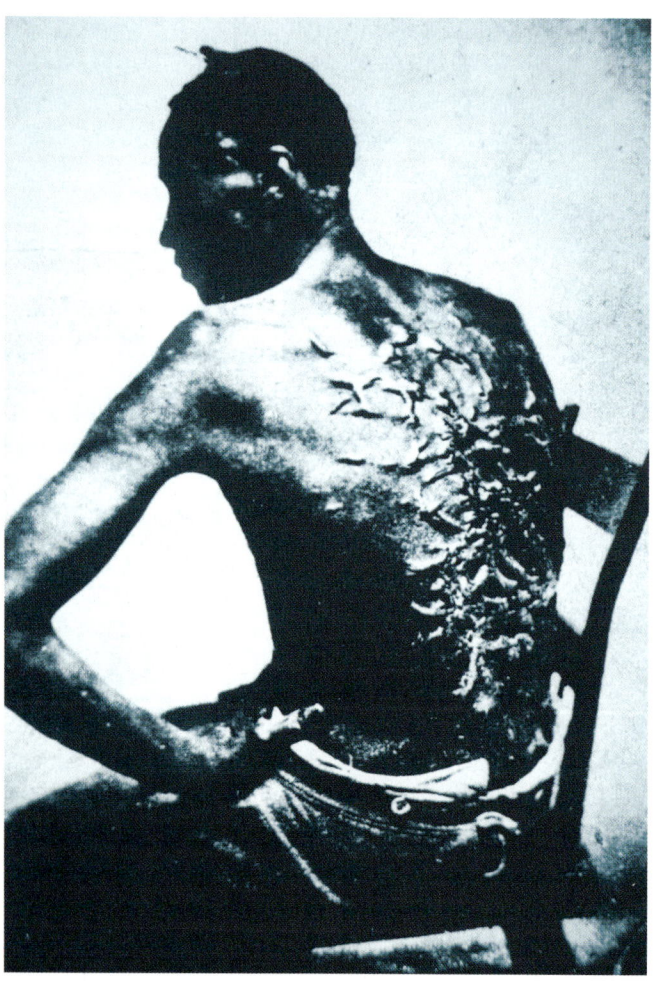

Moses Grandy, who wrote a book about his experiences as a slave in America, *Life of Moses Grandy; Late a Slave* in 1843, described what happened when a slave ran away:

"They hide themselves during the day in the woods and swamps; at night they travel, crossing rivers by swimming, or by boats they may chance to meet with, and passing over hills and meadows which they do not know; in these dangerous journeys they are guided by the north-star, for they only know that the land of freedom is in the north."

◄ *Slaves, such as this man, faced the wrath of their owners every day. The back of this man is heavily scarred from repeated whippings.*

Resisting on the plantation

Slaves could also resist their masters by working more slowly than they were meant to, or by playing 'dumb' – pretending not to understand instructions. Some slaves stole from plantations or broke farm machinery to reduce the profits of the owners. Herbs were sometimes made into poisons and given to the slave owner in his food. Another way for enslaved Africans to resist was to keep their old names, sing traditional African songs, play African drums and speak African languages together. The churches that they attended also blended traditional African ideas about religion with Christian ideas.

◀ *This engraving shows a runaway slave attempting to hide from the slave hunters.*

Underground Railroad

The Underground Railroad was a secret network of routes that many escaped slaves took from the south of the USA to get to Canada. Upper Canada had introduced the Slave Act in 1793 which saw the gradual abolition of slavery until the British Slavery Abolition Act 1833 made slavery illegal in parts of the British Empire. The Underground Railroad was made up of different safe houses, meeting points and transportation provided by 'conductors' who wanted to help the escaping slaves. The conductors came from many different backgrounds, including former slaves, white abolitionists and Native Americans. Harriet Tubman was a slave who escaped to freedom and spent many years rescuing over 70 slaves using the Underground Railroad.

Slave revolts

Revolts, or uprisings, were often the most violent ways for enslaved Africans to resist slavery. The prospect of slave uprisings terrified plantation owners, so any unrest was quickly stopped. But even unsuccessful revolts had a serious impact – they encouraged slaves to feel that their freedom could be achieved.

▲ *This statue in Barbados is of Bussa, and symbolises breaking the chains of slavery.*

Bussa's rebellion

On 14 April 1816, a large rebellion took place on Bayley's Plantation in Barbados. Led by a slave called Bussa, the rebels aimed to take over the island and replace the governor with their own leader, Washington Franklin. Bussa led 400 slaves into battle with the plantation owners, setting the sugar cane fields on fire. Soon the rebellion spread across the island. Eventually, soldiers from the West India Regiment were bought in to crush the uprising and Bussa was killed. Although Bussa's rebellion did not succeed, it gave hope to slaves on Barbados that they would one day be free. However the reprisals were severe; 144 slaves were executed and 123 sentenced to transportation. In total it has been estimated that 1,000 slaves were killed or executed as a result of Bussa's rebellion. A single white person was killed.

Nat Turner's rebellion

Nat Turner (1800–1831) was born into slavery and grew up in Virginia, USA, where he learned to read and write. Turner became very religious and preached the Bible. He believed he had a

▲ *This American engraving shows the slave rebellion led by Nat Turner in 1831.*

Did you know?

One of the earliest known slave revolts – The Servants' Plot – happened in 1663 in Virginia, USA. A group of African slaves, Native Americans and white indentured servants (people contracted to work for a set time) attempted to overthrow their masters. But a fellow servant betrayed the plotters and several were executed.

mission from God to lead a revolt to free the slaves in Virginia, so he and seven close friends planned an uprising in 1831. They moved from house to house on the plantations, freeing the enslaved Africans and killing the white slave owners. In total, 55 white people were killed during the uprising, which lasted for two days before soldiers crushed it. Nat Turner escaped and hid for two months before being captured and executed. After the Turner rebellion, slave owners were always afraid that they could be overthrown – and enslaved Africans had a martyr and a hero.

▲ *In this engraving, Nat Turner (in the blue top) talks with fellow slaves in an 'imagined' scene.*

Slaves in Jamaica who had escaped and claimed their freedom were called Cimarrons (the Spanish word for 'wild') or Maroons. In the mid-16th century, the British fought against the Spanish for control of the Caribbean and made a deal with the Maroons to fight with them.

Queen Nanny

After the Maroons helped Sir Francis Drake fight the Spanish, Drake was presented with a medallion from Queen Elizabeth to commemorate his alliance with the Maroons. However, the good relationship between the British and the Maroons was short-lived. When the British captured Jamaica in 1655, there were a number of slave revolts led by

▲ *An image of Nanny of the Maroons appears on the Jamaican $500 note.*

the Maroons. There are few accurate sources that provide evidence about one of the most famous leaders of the Maroons, a woman known as Nanny. Although there is little doubt she existed, it is not known how much she took part in the fight against the British. It is believed that Nanny was an Asante (from Ghana) and lived in a Maroon community in the Blue Mountains (known as 'Nanny Town') where she raised crops. The Maroons began to raid the local towns, stealing food, setting fire to the sugar cane and liberating slaves from the plantations.

The Maroon Wars

The British got so fed up with the attacks by the Maroons that they sent in the army to stop them. The first Maroon war started in 1729 and lasted for over 10 years. 'Nanny Town' was well-protected as it was high up in the mountains with only a single path leading to it. This meant that the Maroons could see the British coming and could use guerrilla tactics to defeat them. In one story, Nanny helped to camouflage her men with branches and twigs, and made them stand still so that the British couldn't see them and would be surprised by the attack.

▲ *This photograph from c.1908 shows people in the Maroon community.*

Legends of Nanny

Many legends are connected with Nanny, some of which are more believable than others. One story tells how Nanny was so powerful, she could catch bullets in her hands. Another story came from the time when the Maroons were close to starvation. Nanny heard voices from her ancestors telling her not to give up and the following morning she found some pumpkin seeds in her pocket. The seeds were planted and within weeks there were enough pumpkins for the Maroons to eat. Today one of the hills near Nanny Town is called 'Pumpkin Hill'.

Even after Nanny's death, in around 1733, the Maroons were strong enough to keep fighting against the British. They were eventually granted their independence in 1739 with their own lands in the east of Jamaica.

▲ *This engraving from 1759 shows the type of sudden attack launched by the Maroons.*

Toussaint L'Ouverture's rebellion

IN DEPTH

The most successful rebellion against slavery in the Caribbean came on the island of St-Domingue, led by Pierre Dominique Toussaint L'Ouverture. The rebellion raged between 1791 and 1804 and ended with complete independence for St-Domingue after the defeat of armies from France, Spain and Britain.

French education

Toussaint Bréda was born into slavery on the French colony of St-Domingue. He was fortunate to have an owner who taught him to read and write, and eventually granted him freedom when he was 33.

Toussaint was an intelligent man who read widely about new ideas of freedom and equality emerging from the French Revolution in 1789. He believed that enslaved Africans should have the same rights as people in France.

The military leader

Toussaint fought against the French in St-Domingue in 1791, after the French Revolutionary government (which had overthrown the royal family) had gone back on its promises to abolish slavery. He became an important military leader, and changed his name to L'Ouverture (which means 'the one who finds an opening'). In command of 4,000 troops, he showed great skill in military tactics and planning.

◀ *Toussaint L'Ouverture on horseback after he became a general.*

▲ *Toussaint L'Ouverture and his men are defeated by the French at Ravine aux Couleuvres.*

In 1794, the French government abolished slavery in the French Caribbean. As a result, Toussaint joined the French army and in just one week his troops won seven battles against the British and the Spanish. By 1797, Toussaint was the effective leader of St-Domingue. He signed a trading treaty with Britain and the USA, and freed the slaves on the Spanish island of Santo Domingo (Dominican Republic).

Toussaint and Napoleon

When Napoleon came to power in France in 1799, he was pressurised by plantation owners to reintroduce slavery. In 1802, a French army landed in St-Domingue, captured Toussaint and took him to France. He was put in prison in Paris, before being moved to a mountain fortress, where the conditions were so bad that Toussaint died of pneumonia in April, 1803. While on board the ship sailing to France, Toussaint said:

"In overthrowing me you have cut down in St-Domingue only the trunk of the tree of liberty, it will spring up again from the roots, for they are many and they are deep."

Toussaint was proved correct. In 1804 the French left the island – renamed Haiti. Haiti became the first independent black republic outside of Africa.

◄ *The death of Toussaint L'Ouverture in France, 1803.*

The resistance shown by Africans to their enslavement reinforced the belief among many campaigners in Britain that slavery was wrong and should be abolished. The abolitionist movement that developed in the late 18th century was led by people such as Olaudah Equiano, Granville Sharp, Thomas Clarkson, Elizabeth Heyrick and William Wilberforce.

▲ This pro-slavery illustration presents the perceived happiness of enslaved people alongside the unhappiness of a poverty-stricken family in 1830s England.

New voices

The abolition movement was the first time that a mass movement of people from different backgrounds and from all over the British Isles came together to campaign for a single cause. The important contribution from women to the abolitionist cause should also be recognised, as it represented the first time that women had participated in public on such a large scale.

It is also important to acknowledge the contribution that Africans made to their own liberation, such as Equiano, Ottobah Cugoano and Mary Prince.

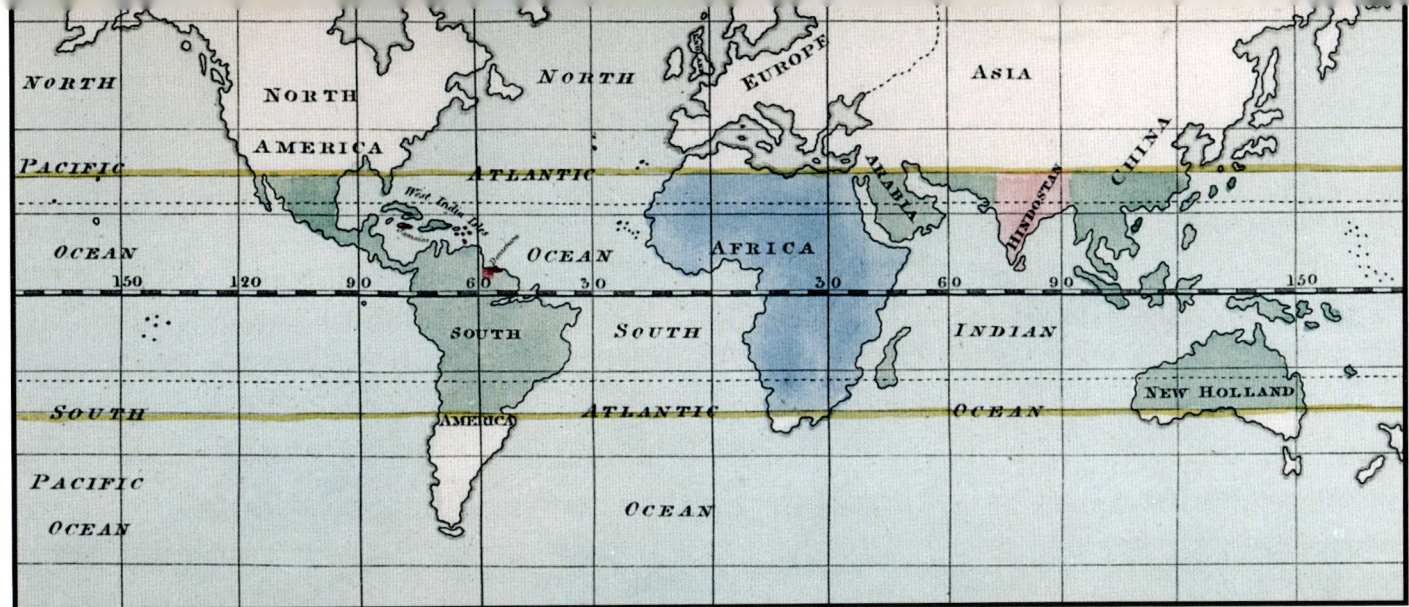

▲ This chart was used to support changes to the enslavement of Africans. It was argued that the slave trade prevented land in Africa from being used to grow valuable crops, such as sugar cane.

Leading African

Leading African abolitionist, Olaudah Equiano, funded the publication and distribution of his autobiography. His supporters included Members of Parliament (MPs) and the Prince of Wales. Equiano considered himself an English gentleman; he married an English lady and had two daughters. This English identity also made his arguments against slavery in the British Empire even stronger.

Act of 1807

The 1807 Act abolishing the slave trade did not bring practical slavery to an end — in reality it did not even end slave trading. Enslaved Africans continued to work and be transported across the Atlantic, and conditions on the plantations did not improve. It was not until the Slavery Abolition Act of 1833 that slavery itself was abolished in some British territories (the Caribbean, Canada and Cape Town).

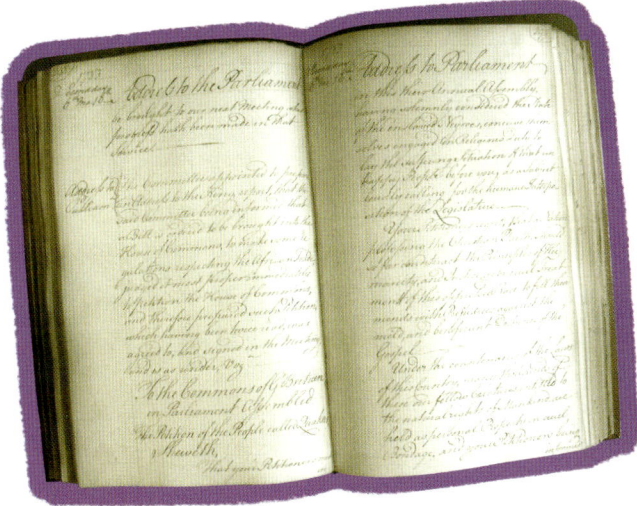

▲ A 1783 anti-slavery petition.

Campaign methods

The campaign methods of the abolitionists were very effective. Mass petitions gathered hundreds of thousands of signatures, while sugar boycotts (see page 33) cut the profits of the plantation owners. Tireless work was done by people such as Thomas Clarkson, who toured Britain revealing the horrors of the slave trade. This was matched by the pressure MPs such as William Wilberforce, and later Sir Thomas Buxton, brought to bear on Parliament.

Africans in Britain

While the vast majority of enslaved Africans were taken across the Atlantic, there were still African slaves in Britain from the middle of the 17th century until the abolition of slavery in 1833, and in some cases afterwards. The court cases bought by Africans, especially the Somerset Case, were critically important in changing the legal landscape at a time when the supporters of slavery were very powerful.

Katherine Auker

An early example of an African attempting to use the law to gain freedom happened in 1690. Katherine Auker, who had been brought to England on a trip from Barbados by her owner Robert Rich, had herself baptised. This meant that as a Christian, it should have been impossible for Rich to keep Auker as a slave. He threw her out onto the streets, but refused to give up ownership of her and prevented her from finding work elsewhere. Auker took the case to court and won the right to get paid work. However, her victory was temporary – she was taken back into slavery when Rich returned once more to Britain from Barbados to claim her.

◄ *It was not uncommon for plantation owners to have young female slaves in attendance.*

The Somerset Case

James Somerset was a slave who had run away from his owners when they brought him to Britain from Jamaica. He was recaptured and imprisoned on a ship due to return to Jamaica. However, friends rescued him and the case was bought to court. On 22 June 1792, Chief Justice Lord Mansfield delivered his judgement in the Somerset Case, which stopped any person (including slaves) being removed from England against their will. According to a report in a London newspaper, 200 black people gathered a few days later:

"…at a public house in Westminster, to celebrate the triumph which their brother Somerset had obtained over Mr Stewart, his master."

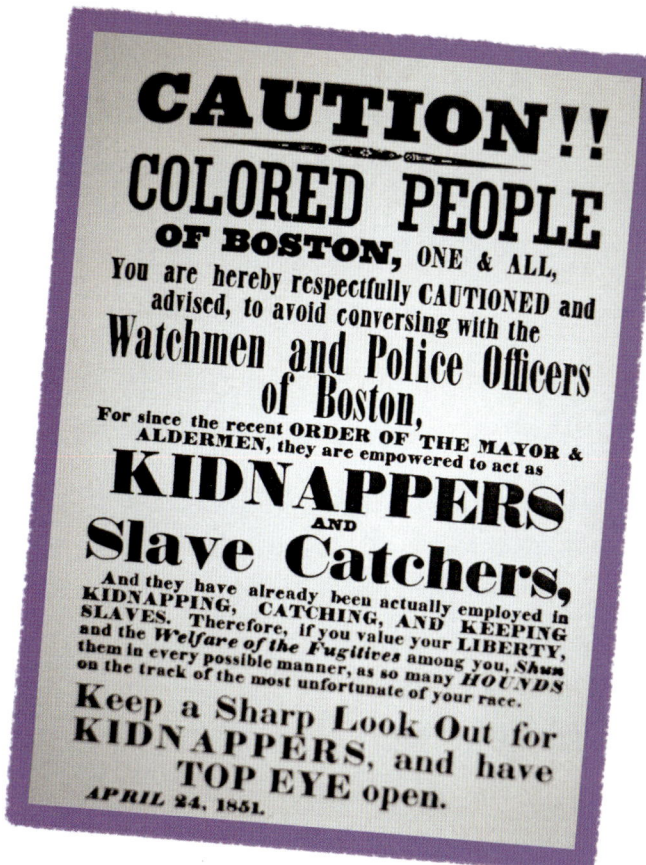

▲ An anti-slavery poster by Reverend Theodore Parker, 1851.

African-Britons campaign

One of the most overlooked aspects of the struggle to end the slave trade, and slavery itself, has been the contribution of Africans in Britain and the Americas to their own liberation. Leading African-Briton abolitionists, such as Olaudah Equiano and Ottabah Cugoano (1757–unknown), along with others, joined organisations such as the Sons of Africa to campaign against slavery. They wrote letters to newspapers, published books against the slave trade and supported the Parliamentary campaign around the country.

▶ This is believed to be the only portrait of Ottabah Cugoano (right). He is shown serving fruit to Richard Cosway and his wife.

Olaudah Equiano the abolitionist

Born in West Africa in 1745, Olaudah Equiano was captured and sold into slavery at the age of eleven. His first owner was a Royal Navy captain, who brought him to Greenwich, London, where he was taught to read and write by the Guerin sisters, the captain's relatives. Equiano eventually bought his freedom for £40 earned from small trading, and spent the rest of his life campaigning against the slave trade.

▲ *A portrait of Olaudah Equiano c.1789.*

The campaigner

Equiano had established himself as an important and effective campaigner against slavery even before he published his autobiography *The Interesting Narrative of Olaudah Equiano, or Gustavus Vassa, the African* in 1789.

He was a regular letter writer and in particular wrote many letters to newspapers around the country. Equiano argued passionately that slavery was wrong and that it was against the teachings of the Bible:

"Surely this traffic [of slaves] cannot be good, which spreads like a disease and damages every thing it touches … [which denies the] right[s] of mankind, equality and independency, and gives one man [power] over his fellows which God could never intend! For it raises the owner to a [position] as far above man as it depresses the slave below it."

Call for free trade

Equiano also argued that Britain could make more money from trading with Africa instead of enslaving her people:

▲ *Enslaved Africans in the hold of a slave trading ship.*

"I doubt not, if a system of [trade] was established (set up) in Africa, the demand for [British goods e.g. cloth, pots] would most rapidly increase, as the [Africans] will adopt the British fashions, manners, customs etc… A commercial [relationship] with Africa opens up an inexhaustible source of wealth to the manufacturing interests of Great Britain … the manufacturers of this country … will … have [many jobs] by supplying the African markets."

▲ *New Hall tea set c. 1800, just one example of goods being produced in Britain at the time.*

Equiano's book was the first to show the reality of the Transatlantic Slave Trade, including evidence of the Middle Passage, and the terrible conditions faced by slaves in the Caribbean and southern United States.

The book tour

Equiano was able to fund the publication and distribution of his autobiography by collecting subscriptions. By the time the 9th edition was published in 1794, over 1,000 people had subscribed to the book including the Prince of Wales and many MPs. This income also meant Equiano could travel to speak at meetings of the Society for the Abolition of the Slave Trade (see pages 30–31) and other abolitionist groups. Equiano died in 1797 aged 52, ten years before the slave trade was abolished. However, he made an enormous contribution to the abolitionist cause. Equiano's autobiography was translated into many different languages and has barely been out of print since its publication over 200 years ago.

Society for the Abolition of the Slave Trade

The first meeting of the Society for the Abolition of the Slave Trade took place on 22 May 1787, when 12 men met in a London printing shop to commit themselves to the abolitionist cause. From small beginnings emerged one of the most effective campaigning groups of the modern era.

Stopping the trade

The driving forces behind the Society were Granville Sharp and Thomas Clarkson, supported by William Wilberforce and the African abolitionist Olaudah Equiano. The initial campaign was against the slave trade rather than the practice of slavery.

The group felt this was a more realistic target that would have more success in Parliament, where many MPs had interests connected with the slave trade. The campaign to ban slavery itself and free enslaved Africans would come later.

Granville Sharp

Granville Sharp was born in Durham in 1735. He became known as a 'defender of the Negro' for his work supporting runaway slaves and on the case of the slave ship *Zong*, where 133 enslaved Africans had been thrown overboard. Sharp became knowledgeable in the law relating to slavery, and used this to great effect in the Somerset Case (see page 27). He was an original member of the Society for the Abolition of the Slave Trade. His works included 'A Representation of the Injustice and Dangerous Tendency of Tolerating Slavery', in 1769 – the first anti-slavery writing to be published in England. Sharp died in 1813, still campaigning for the end of slavery.

▲ *Granville Sharp (right) became known for his defence of Black rights.*

Thomas Clarkson

Another original member of the Society, Thomas Clarkson (1760–1846), collected evidence used to promote the anti-slavery cause. One of the most powerful tools Clarkson used was a set of drawings of the slave ship *Brookes*. These images (right) showed how enslaved Africans were transported in terrible conditions.

Clarkson travelled around Britain to spread the abolitionist message, even going to the slave-trading cities of Bristol and Liverpool at personal risk. Clarkson wrote pamphlets and letters in favour of abolition throughout his life. In 1807, he campaigned for the Abolition of the Slave Trade Act. He died in 1846 having seen the Abolition and Emancipation Acts passed by Parliament.

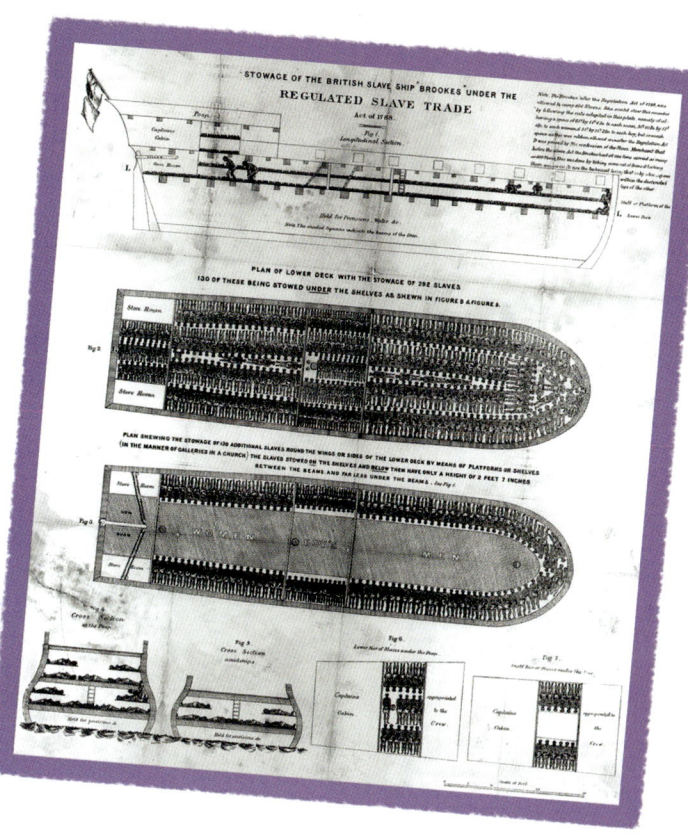

▲ *Diagrams showing the capacity of the British slave ship* Brookes.

▲ *Thomas Clarkson with samples of goods from Africa (right).*

Did you know?

Bristol and Liverpool were the main British ports involved in the Transatlantic Slave Trade. From 1697 to 1807, over 2,000 ships sailed from Bristol to the West Indies with slaves, and the profits from the trade brought the city great wealth. Slave trading was also a main factor in Liverpool's prosperity in the 18th century. Almost 1.5 million Africans were transported across the Atlantic on slave ships built or repaired in Liverpool.

Am I not a man and a brother?

The campaign against the slave trade and slavery kept its focus over many years, with dedicated people lending their time and talents. Along with famous contributors, vast numbers of people from all corners of Britain united to fight for a single cause. Abolitionists used many tactics to put pressure on Parliament to support abolition. These included petitions, boycotts and mass marketing techniques including creating their own badge and logo.

Signing petitions

The first petitions to end the slave trade were presented to Parliament in 1787 and by the end of that year over 100 had been collected with over 60,000 names on them. By 1792, this had increased to more than 500 petitions with an estimated 400,000 signatures. These petitions were signed by ordinary working people around the country who opposed the treatment of enslaved Africans. The petitions worked to increase the pressure on members of Parliament to support bills put forward to the House of Commons to abolish the slave trade.

▲ *Anti-slavery meetings were held to promote the rights of Black Africans.*

▲ *This Wedgwood medallion shows a slave with the words: 'Am I Not a Man and a Brother?'*

Branding logo

One of the most effective ways of spreading the abolitionist message, particularly to a population where most struggled to read and write, was to use images and slogans. The famous pottery businessman Josiah Wedgwood was a supporter of the campaign. He agreed to manufacture cameos (oval pieces of jewellery or pottery) featuring the image and slogan of the Society for the Abolition of the Slave Trade – an African man kneeling down in chains with the words 'Am I not a man and a brother?' underneath. A later version also appeared with the words 'Am I not a woman and a sister?' The images appeared on many different every day items including teacups, brooches, bracelets and even cufflinks.

Anti-sugar boycotts

When the first attempt to outlaw the slave trade failed in 1791, the abolitionists tried to find a different way to apply pressure. Now it used the economic power that abolitionists held. As so much money was made from the sugar industry, which survived almost entirely using the labour of enslaved Africans, a boycott of slave-grown sugar was launched. Within a year, over 400,000 people were boycotting sugar from the Caribbean and instead were buying sugar from India. It has been estimated that sales of sugar fell by nearly a half at the height of the boycott.

One of the most striking aspects of the sugar boycotts was the contribution made by women to the campaign, at a time when their participation in public life was limited.

▲ *A jug with an anti-slavery message produced as part of the anti-slavery campaign.*

The Abolition Acts

Towards the end of the 18th century, pressure was growing to bring the Transatlantic Slave Trade to an end. The activities of the abolitionists, including hundreds of petitions, letters and meetings combined with the anti-sugar boycotts, led to the parliamentary campaign to stop the trade in enslaved Africans. William Wilberforce (1759–1833) was the most famous MP to support abolition. He was responsible for introducing many bills in order to achieve this aim.

William Wilberforce

Born in Hull in 1759, William Wilberforce became the MP for Hull in 1780. He became friends with Thomas Clarkson and Granville Sharp, and was persuaded by their arguments that the slave trade should be abolished. The first abolition bill was introduced with a four-hour speech by Wilberforce in 1791 but was defeated. The powerful West India Lobby – the supporters of the plantation owners who were making huge profits from slavery – were not going to give up easily. Wilberforce continued to introduce abolition bills every year until slowly the MPs were won over.

▲ *A portrait of William Wilberforce.*

Slave Trade Act 1807

The tide turned in the abolitionists' favour in 1806 with the election of a new Prime Minister, William Grenville, who was a keen supporter of abolition. When a vote was taken on the Slave Trade Abolition Bill in January 1807, it was first passed in the House of Lords by 100 votes to 34, and then passed in the House of Commons by 283 votes to 16. The bill received the Royal Assent on 25 March 1807. The British slave trade was abolished, and as a result, British ships and people had to stop trading in enslaved Africans.

▲ *A procession in England, 1808, after the ban on the Transatlantic Slave Trade.*

Abolition of Slavery Act 1833

Ironically, one of the consequences of the abolition of the slave trade was an increase in the profits made by plantation owners. This was because many slave traders had found profitable ways to break the new law. The conditions on the plantations did not improve and there was an increase in the number of rebellions. The idea that slavery would be abolished gradually was becoming less respected, and pressure increased for its immediate abolition, particularly from Elizabeth Heyrick and women's anti-slavery societies (see pages 36–37).

Wilberforce retired from the House of Commons in 1825 and the leadership of the parliamentary abolitionist movement passed to Sir Thomas Buxton. The 1832 Reform Act led to an increase in the number of abolitionist MPs and in the same year, a large-scale rebellion in Jamaica also convinced MPs that the time had come to end slavery. The Abolition of Slavery Act was passed in July 1833, which outlawed slavery in the Caribbean, Canada, Cape Town and Mauritius.

▲ *In this scene from the 1832 Jamaica rebellion, freed slaves attack the plantation house.*

Elizabeth Heyrick, a Quaker from Leicester, published a pamphlet in 1824 called 'Immediate not Gradual Abolition'. This was a radical and powerful argument that called for the end of slavery and the continuation of the sugar boycotts that "may save (England) the annual tax of THREE MILLIONS now paid in the direct support of slavery". Heyrick travelled around Leicester visiting grocers' shops to check whether they were selling 'slave-grown sugar'.

Women abolitionists

In 1825, Heyrick, along with many other women activists in the abolition movement, attended a meeting in Birmingham and challenged the leadership to explain why women had been excluded from any positions of authority in the Anti-Slavery Society (which had replaced the Society for the Abolition of the Slave Trade). William Wilberforce (see pages 34—35), in particular, felt that women were unsuited to involvement in the organisation "[F]or ladies to meet, to publish, to go from house to house stirring up petitions – these appear to me proceedings unsuited to the female character [as it is said in the Bible]."

▲ No images of Elizabeth Heyrick exist. Shown here is Anne Knight, who was also a Quaker and an anti-slavery campaigner.

▶ A report from the Female Society for the Relief of British Negro Slaves.

THE
FIRST REPORT
OF
THE FEMALE SOCIETY,
[1825-26]
FOR
BIRMINGHAM, WEST-BROMWICH, WEDNESBURY, WALSALL,
AND THEIR RESPECTIVE NEIGHBOURHOODS,
FOR THE RELIEF OF
British Negro Slaves.

BIRMINGHAM:
Printed at the Office of Richard Peart, 28, Bull-street.
1826.

Wilberforce even went as far as trying to suppress Heyrick's pamphlet. As a consequence, Heyrick and others established the Birmingham Ladies Society for the Relief of Negro Slaves, and soon there were over 70 women's anti-slavery societies around the country.

Immediate action

Heyrick argued passionately that slavery should be abolished immediately and claimed that Wilberforce and Thomas Clarkson were taking far too long to achieve that goal. She even went as far as saying that, "the abolitionists have shown a great deal too much politeness and accommodation towards (the plantation owners)...Why petition Parliament at all, to do that for us, which... we can do more speedily and effectually for ourselves?"

Financial pressure

In 1830, a resolution was put forward at the meeting of the Anti-Slavery Society calling for immediate abolition. In order to make this demand more effective, Heyrick also suggested that the women's anti-slavery societies should withdraw their funds (around 20% of all donations) from the Anti-Slavery Society if it wasn't met. Her pressure was effective and the Anti-Slavery Society now started to push for immediate abolition. Within three years, slavery had been abolished in parts of the British Empire. Sadly, Elizabeth Heyrick did not live long enough to see the fruits of her dedication. She died in 1831 at the age of 61.

▲ *A banner for the Anti-Slavery Society hanging in a street in Hull, England.*

The legacy of the slave trade

The supporters of the 1807 Act believed that the consequence of the abolition of the slave trade would be an end to slavery. However, it soon became apparent that this was not happening. There were many loopholes in the Act, which meant that trading in slaves continued and profits from slave-produced goods were actually increasing.

Abolition effectiveness

Historians have estimated that over 2.5 million Africans were transported across the Atlantic (mainly to Brazil and Cuba) between 1811 and 1870. This was in spite of the British government trying to persuade other countries including France, the Netherlands and Spain to stop trading slaves. The Royal Navy's West Africa

▲ *A Royal Navy launch chases a slaving ship off the east coast of Africa c.1876.*

Squadron also worked to capture ships still carrying slaves.

The 1833 Act brought an end to slavery in the Caribbean, Canada and Cape Town, although not immediately, and not in the rest of the British Empire.

Beyond Britain

Although slavery had been banned in many US states (called 'free states') as early as 1787, slavery continued to exist in the southern United States until 1865 when the American Civil War finally ended the practice. In Cuba, slavery continued until 1882 and in Brazil until 1888. The British still kept between 5 and 10 million slaves in India until slavery was abolished in 1843. The final act of abolition in the British Empire was not until 1936 in Nigeria.

▲ *These troops, from the 4th US Colored Infantry, fought during the American Civil War.*

Did you know?

A significant aspect of the 1833 Act was that £20 million was provided by the government to the slave owners as compensation for their loss of earnings. To this day, not a single penny has been paid to the enslaved Africans or their families for their suffering.

Slavery today

It would also be wrong to think that slavery does not exist today. There are slaves all around the world ranging from child workers in Asia to an estimated 800,000 men and women in Niger in West Africa. Even in Haiti, the home of Toussaint L'Ouverture and the first Caribbean country to abolish slavery, an estimated 200,000 children are being used as domestic slaves according to a recent report by the BBC. Organisations such as Anti-slavery are still fighting the same cause that Olaudah Equiano, Thomas Clarkson, Granville Sharp, William Wilberforce, Elizabeth Heyrick and thousands of others fought over two centuries ago.

▼ *An enslaved girl in modern-day Niger, Africa. Her bracelets identify her as a slave.*

Timeline – Resistance and Abolition

1441 The first record of Africans being enslaved and taken to Portugal

1562 Sir John Hawkins becomes the first Englishman to trade in African slaves

1624 Queen Nzinga challenges Portuguese slave traders in Angola

1729 The first Maroon wars in Jamaica

1730 Slave revolt on *The Little George*

1739 The Maroons are given their own lands in the east of Jamaica

1745 Olaudah Equiano born in Essaka in the kingdom of Benin (now Ghana)

1750–1800 The height of the Transatlantic Slave Trade – at least 3 million Africans are transported to the Americas

1770 Slave revolts on board the *Unity* from Liverpool

1772 The Somerset Case prevents enslaved Africans from being kidnapped in England and returned to the Caribbean

1776 The United States of America becomes independent of Great Britain

1787 Society for the Abolition of the Slave Trade founded

1789 Olaudah Equiano publishes his autobiography *The Interesting Narrative...*

1797 Toussaint L'Ouverture becomes leader of St-Domingue (later renamed Haiti)

1804 Haiti declares independence and abolishes slavery

1807 The abolition of the slave trade. West Africa Squadron of the Royal Navy formed to stop slave ships leaving Africa

1816 Bussa's rebellion

1817–18 France and Holland abolish slave trading. Spain and Portugal sign treaties with Britain to stop slave trading.

1831 Nat Turner's rebellion

1833 The abolition of slavery in the British Empire

1839 The *Amistad* Uprising

1865 Abolition of slavery in the United States of America with the 13th amendment to the Constitution

1936 Britain abolishes slavery in northern Nigeria

Key

- Resistance

- Abolition

Websites and Bibliography

Websites

http:/www.blackhistory4schools.co.uk/ slavetrade/ An excellent set of resources related to the Transatlantic Slave Trade, resistance and abolition.

http://www.brycchancarey.com/ Brycchan Carey's excellent website about slavery,

An Interesting Narrative....

http://www.bbc.co.uk/history/british/ abolition/ Comprehensive guide to the abolition of the slave trade.

http://www.nationalarchives.gov.uk/edu cation/lessons/bussas-rebellion Online lesson about Bussa's rebellion.

Bibliography

Equiano O, *The Interesting Narrative of Olaudah Equiano or Gustavus Vassa the African*, Penguin, 1996

Foster N, *Out of Slavery*, Redcliffe Publishing, 2004

Fryer P, *Staying Power, the History of Black People in Britain*, Pluto Press, 1984

Hinds D, *Black Peoples of the Americas*, Collins Educational, 1992

Hosking T, *Black People in Britain 1650–1850*, Macmillan, 1984

Lester J, *To be a Slave*, Puffin Books, 1998

Rees B and Sherwood M, *Black Peoples of the Americas*, Heinemann, 1992

Rees R, *Britain and the Slave Trade*, Heinemann, 1995

Sherwood K and Sherwood M, *Britain, the slave trade and slavery from 1562 to the 1880s*, Savannah Press, 2007

Sherwood M, After Abolition, *Britain and the Slave Trade since 1807*, I B Tauris & Co, 2007

Smith N, *Black Peoples of the Americas*, OUP, 1992

Torrington A et al (Ed), *Equiano, Enslavement, Resistance and Abolition*, Equiano Society and Birmingham Museums and Art Gallery, 2007

Walvin J, *Slavery to Freedom*, Pitkin Publishing, 2007

Glossary

Abolition
To put an end to something completely.

Abolitionist
Someone who wanted to abolish the slavery of Black Africans.

Alliance
A formal friendship made between countries or peoples.

Americas
The word used to describe all the lands of both North and South America.

Barricade
A temporary defensive barrier.

Boycott
Refuse to have anything to do with a product or a country.

Calvary
The hill outside Jerusalem where Jesus Christ was crucified.

Christianity
The religion based on the teachings of Jesus Christ.

Culture
The arts, beliefs and traditions of a particular society.

Emancipation
To be set free.

Grating
A criss-cross of metal or wood placed over an opening to let air circulate or to prevent escape.

Guerrilla
A type of fighting carried out by people who do not belong to a normal army. Guerrilla forces tend to use surprise attacks and sabotage – planned destruction of supplies and materials – to fight the enemy.

Hatch
A movable covering over an opening or door, especially in the deck of a ship.

Insurrection
A word for an uprising or rebellion.

Maroons
From the Spanish word *cimarron*, meaning 'wild' or 'untamed'. The Maroons were escaped slaves living in Jamaica's mountain areas.

Middle Passage
The part of the Transatlantic Slave Trade, where enslaved Africans were taken from Africa to the Americas. The journey lasted between 6 and 8 weeks and many Africans died from the terrible conditions.

Negroes

Word used to describe black people from Africa – now considered by many to be offensive.

Overseer

Large landowners used an overseer to make the slaves work as hard as possible on the plantations.

Plantation

Large farms that the enslaved Africans were forced to work on, growing crops such as sugar, tobacco and cotton.

Slavery

When someone is forced to work for another person and loses all of their freedom and rights.

Subscription

A sum of money paid for receiving a magazine, newspaper or membership of a club.

Sugar industry

The growing, harvesting, processing and selling of sugar, particularly sugar cane.

Transatlantic Slave Trade

The name given to the enslavement and forced removal of millions of Africans from Africa to the Americas between the 16th and 19th centuries.

Transportation

To send a criminal abroad to a foreign country as a punishment. Once they'd arrived they had to work for a set amount of time, or even for the rest of their lives, on government projects such as road building.

Treadmill

A machine that is made to rotate by the walking action of a person or animal.

Underground Railroad

The network of safe houses and people which helped slaves to escape from the southern USA to 'free' areas in North America.

Watch

The person who has to keep a look out for danger, especially at night.

West Indies

Large group of islands in the Caribbean Sea and including Barbados, Jamaica, Antigua and the Turks and Caicos Islands.

Index

These are the lists of contents for the titles in *Black History*:

ST - INDIEN
und
RAL - AMERIKA
eichnet von Hermann Berghaus.

Maaſsstab 1 : 9 250 000

50 Deutsche Meilen, 15 = 1°
200 Geogr. See Meilen, 60 = 1°
Englische Statute Miles, 69,12 = 1°

Schrift Erklärung:
STADT über 100 000
STADT 50 000
Stadt 20 000
Stadt 10 000
Stadt 5 000
Kleinere Stadt

Europaeische Colonien:
Britische
Niederländische
Schwedische
Dänische
Französische
Spanische

ISTHMUS
von
NICARAGUA
im doppelten Maaſsstabe der
Hauptkarte.

ISTHMUS
von
PANAMÁ
im fünffachen Maaſs
der Hauptkarte.

BAHAMA INSELN

HAITI   S. DOMINGO
Hispaniola
REPUBLIK DOMINICAN

PUERTO RICO

ANTILLEN   KLEINE   ODER INSELN ÜBER DEM WINDE

ANTILLEN

ISCHES   MEER

INSELN UNTER DEM WINDE

WEST-INDIEN
und
CENTRAL-AMERIKA

gezeichnet von Hermann Berghaus.

Maaßstab = $\frac{1}{9\,250\,000}$

Deutsche Meilen, 15 = 1°
Geogr. See Meilen, 60 = 1°
Englische Statute Miles, 69,12 = 1°

ISTHMUS
von
NICARAGUA
im doppelten Maaßstabe der Hauptkarte.

Schrift Erklärung:
- ● STADT über 100 000 Einwohner
- ● STADT 50 000
- ● Stadt 20 000
- ● Stadt 10 000
- ● Stadt 5000
- ● Kleinere Stadt

Europaeische Colonien:
- Britische
- Niederländische
- Schwedische
- Dänische
- Französische
- Spanische